The Broken Flower Pot

Story by Annette Smith
Illustrations by Meredith Thomas

Katie kicked the ball to Joe.

"Look out, Joe," she shouted.
"Here it comes."

The ball went way up
over the fence,
and into the garden next door.

Crash!

Joe and Katie ran to the fence.

"Look at Sally's flower pot!"
said Joe.
"The ball has broken it!"

"Look at the flowers, too,"
said Katie.
"They are all over the grass."

Mum came out.

She saw the broken flower pot
and she saw the flowers.

"Sorry, Mum," said Katie.

They went over to Sally's place,
but she was not at home.

"We will have to get Sally
a new flower pot," said Mum.

103

They went back home.

Joe got an old flower pot

out of the shed.

"We can make this old pot

look like a new one,"

he said.

"We can paint it."

Joe painted the old pot blue.

Katie said,

"The old pot looks good now,

but I can make it look better.

I will paint

some yellow flowers on it."

Mum said,

"You are **very** clever.

We will let the pot

dry in the sun."

"Then we can plant

Sally's flowers again," said Joe.

Sally came home
and saw her new flower pot.
"I love it," she said.